MAKE MONEY WITH BINARY OPTIONS:

THE CALENDS STRATEGY

The Binary Options Speculator Book 2

José Manuel Moreira Batista

Introduction

Every day, self-proclaimed stock market "experts" tell us why the market just went up or down, as if they really knew. So where were they yesterday?

~ Anonymous

Make Money with Binary Options: The Calends Strategy presents the easy-to-follow, complete system to successfully trade with binary options that I use. This system is based on a simple yet extremely powerful idea: what worked in the past is more likely than not to work again in the future.

The system trades only once a month and always uses the same type of binary option. Setting up a trade takes a couple of minutes at most: you just look up in a table if the asset you have chosen to trade is expected to go above or fall below a certain value and how much you should bet. You then log into your binary options broker's platform and enter those parameters. No further action is needed until the end of the month.

Make Money with Binary Options: The Calends Strategy describes a complete trading system, meaning one that comprises both a trading strategy and a money management system. This book starts by describing how the trading strategy is built. It also explains the concept of expectancy and how it is used to gauge if a strategy is worth trading and to rank strategies. The rationale of money management comes next, followed by a detailed explanation on how to place the monthly trade.

I am confident you will find this to be a very useful book. I am always looking for new insights and ideas and welcome any suggestions you may be kind enough to offer to help improve this work.

Trade with common sense, have fun and make profits!

José Manuel Moreira Batista

PS: Readers are entitled to receive a free infographic of The Calends Strategy. To receive yours go to morbat.com/calendsinfo.

What readers say

"This is a great read for anyone who wants to get into the market."

Pukanecz

"I have had some good success with this and I have made some good money."

Matthew

"You need to read this if you want to do some trading with binary options."

Laura Groff

"This is an excellent book for anyone wanting to learn how to get into trading using Binary options"

DC7113

"The book contains valuable information about the system trades and binary options."

Bookreader

Contents

The Calends Trading Strategy

Life is really simple, but we insist on making it complicated.

~ Confucius

If you are like me you like to keep things simple. Let's then start by committing ourselves to only making trades that have worked well in the past. In order words, we only want to engage in high probability trades. For that purpose, we assume that the historical success rate of a trade is the best estimation of its probability of success:

Probability of success = Number of winning trades / Total number of trades

This is sometimes also called the *winning percentage*, *win ratio* or *win%*. The probability of a trade's failure, also called the *loss ratio*, is calculated deducting the win ratio from 1:

Loss ratio = 1 - Win ratio

Note that if a trading strategy has a loss ratio of 90% or even 99%, that does not necessarily means it is unprofitable. The opposite goes for a strategy with a 90% or 99% winning percentage: that information alone is not enough to assess if it is going to be profitable. In order to make that call we must first know the average size of both the winning and the losing trades and combine them in the *reward to risk ratio*.

Reward to Risk ratio = Average Win Amount / Average Loss Amount

Finally, the trade's *expectancy* combines the *reward to risk ratio* and the *win and loss ratios* and tells us if the strategy is profitable in the long run.

Expectancy = Reward to risk x Win ratio - Loss ratio

A strategy with a positive expectancy will earn money in the long run. A strategy with a negative expectancy will lose money and therefore should not be traded. If Strategy A has a higher expectancy value than Strategy B we should prefer trading Strategy A over Strategy B.

Now that we have a logic to look out for trades and a mechanism to assess their profitability potential, we need a specific type of binary option to plug them in. The Calends strategy uses the *Higher/Lower* binary option (the *Raise/Fall* binary option may also be used provided the spot price is below/above the barrier). In this type of trade we choose a *barrier*, a *direction* and an *expiration date*. We then bet if the asset price will be higher or lower than the barrier at the end of the day on the expiration date. We place our trades on the first trading day of each month and select its last trading day as the expiration date. The direction of the trade is determined by what happened more often in the past: if the price rose more often than it fell, the direction will be *Higher*, otherwise it will be *Lower*.

The snapshot below shows a Higher/Lower bet on the German index DAX, placed through our preferred binary options broker, Binary.com.

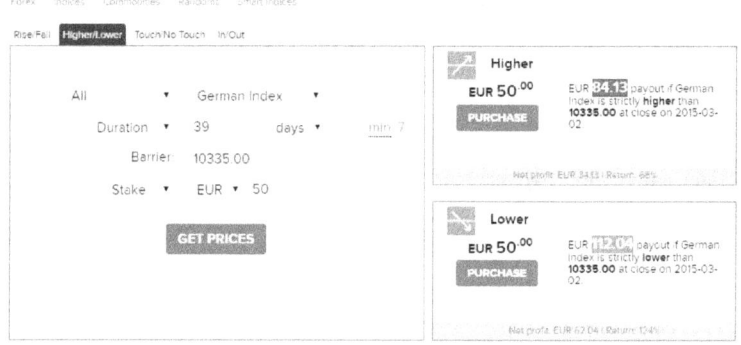

Money Management

You can be young without money, but you can't be old without it.

~ Tennessee Williams

No trading system is complete without a *money management system*. In fact many strategies end up being profitable only because a sound money management system is in place and others fail completely because they lack one. The main idea behind the need for a money management system is to avoid being wiped-out or severely crippled in a single or a few trades. This can happen very easily regardless of the soundness of a trading system. It is inevitable that we will suffer stretches of several losses in a row from time to time. If we bet 10% of our initial capital in every trade and suffer five consecutive losses we will end up with only 50% of the amount we started with. With an average return per trade of 70%, we will then need seven consecutive wins to recover our lost capital and just break-even.

The money management system I prefer is the *Kelly %* (also known as the *Kelly system, Kelly criterion or Kelly formula*). Developed by J.L. Kelly in the 1950s it is proven to do better than any other money management system (if a trade has the same probability of winning or losing each time and the same payout ratio is entered repeatedly).

Kelly % = [W x (R + 1) - 1] / R

In the formula above, W is the average winning percentage of the strategy and R is the average return of the trades. The output of the formula is a number, the percentage of the bankroll we should stake. For example, with W=60% and R=70%, the Kelly % is 2.86%. So if your bankroll is 5000€ the Kelly% is telling you to stake 143€ (5000€ x 2.86%).

Although proven to ultimately fare better than other systems the Kelly formula does not provide a smooth ride and steep drawdowns tend to happen with some frequency.

Should you prefer a lower adrenaline rush, use only half or a fourth of the Kelly % to calculate how much to stake on each trade. Alternatively you could use the *percentage of bankroll method*. Using this system you simply bet a fixed percentage of your bankroll on each trade. That percentage is usually between 2% to 5%. With a bankroll of 5000€ you would therefore stake 100€ (5000€ x 2%) in your next trade.

The Monthly Trade

What we call chaos is just patterns we haven't recognized. What we call random is just patterns we can't decipher.

~ Chuck Palahniuk

As stated before, the Calends strategy is based on identifying recurring monthly upwards or downwards price patterns on an asset price. Let's see how it works using the NASDAQ 100 index as an example. The table below was built using data downloaded for free from Yahoo! Finance.

[1] ^NDX : USA: NASDAQ-100				
[2] <-> Base scenario: 0,0% from opening				
# Years	[3] 24	Assumed return:		[4] 70%
Month	Direction	Win %	Expectancy	Kelly %
January	Higher	69.6%	0.18	7%
February	Lower	54.2%	0.32	6%
March	Higher	66.7%	0.13	5%
April	Higher	54.2%	-0.08	0%
May	Higher	62.5%	0.06	2%
June	Lower	58.3%	0.42	7%
July	Higher	58.3%	-0.01	0%
August	Higher	54.2%	-0.08	0%
September	Higher	62.5%	0.06	2%
October	Higher	70.8%	0.20	7%
November	Higher	66.7%	0.13	5%
December	Higher	62.5%	0.06	2%

Note: this table is for illustration purposes only

1 – *^NDX* is Yahoo!'s ticker for the NASDAQ 100 index.

2 – In a base scenario the barrier is equal to the opening value of the index for the month thus the indication "0% from opening".

3 – The number of years of data used in the calculations was 24. This number is determined by the data availability. Obviously a larger set of data gives more confidence than a smaller set.

4 – The calculations assume that binary trades pay 70% of the staked amount, a fairly common payout. This is relevant for the computation of the trade's expectancy and the Kelly %. If the trade return offered is lower than 70% no trade should be made.

5 – The trade *direction* is either *higher* or *lower*. If the past data shows the asset price going up more often than down then the direction of the trade will be higher, otherwise it will be lower.

6 – This column displays the past success rate in each month for a trade with the direction shown. For example, in past years the NASDAQ 100 closing price at the end of January was higher than the opening price in the first trading day of the month 69.6% of the times. By contrast in February it was lower 54.2% of the times.

7 – This column displays each month's trade expectancy. If a trade's expectancy is positive it is okay to trade. If a trade's expectancy is negative the trade should not be made.

8 – The Kelly % displayed here is one fourth of the calculated Kelly percentage for each trade, which is what I actually use in my own trading.

Placing Trades

Know that everything is in perfect order whether you understand it or not.

~ Valery Satterwhite

Placing a trade is a very straightforward matter. Let's assume you are at the beginning of January and have a bankroll of 5000€. The NASDAQ 100 opens on January 2, the first trading day of the month, with a value of 3576. That opening value will be your barrier for the higher/lower binary option. The trade direction is *higher* and you select the last trading day of January as the ending date of the trade. You use the Kelly % shown to determine the amount to stake: multiplying 7% by 5000€ you bet 350€.

Sadly the NASDAQ 100 closes on January 31 at 3522 so your trade books a loss and your bankroll is now 4650€.

The NASDAQ 100 opens on February at 3524 and you bet 279€ (6% x 4650€) that it will end lower than that for the month. Finishing at 3696 it doesn't! Your bankroll shrinks again to 4371€.

Undeterred you take 3675 as your barrier for March and bet 219€ (5% x 4371€) that the index will end the month higher.

You go on to repeat this process every month...

You might be wondering why I've chosen to exemplify this strategy with a couple of losses, which is hardly the way to get people to be enthusiastic about it. The reason is simple: I want to impress on you that this is a strategy aiming for long-term profits and that you will suffer losses from time to time. In fact, you will have consecutive losses and you might experience severe drawdowns. This strategy requires discipline, patience and perseverance and it is therefore not suited to everyone. It us certainly not the best choice for those hoping to score a quick big win although that can certainly happen. With that out of the way, let's turn on to the most frequently asked questions about the strategy.

Frequently Asked Questions

If you ask me a multiple part question, and half my answers are yes and half are no, I may just average them together and give you a definitive and vague maybe.

~ Jarod Kintz

How do you build the table with the calculations?

The first thing to do is to get the historical price data. Stocks and indices data can be downloaded for free from Yahoo! Finance. It comes in CSV format which is easily imported into Excel and if you are only interested in analyzing a few assets that is all you need. If you want to download data frequently or for a large number of assets you should consider buying specific software. I use and recommend MLDownloader (Windows) and StockXloader (Mac). Both are very reasonably priced and easy to work with. Historical data for Forex pairs is not available from Yahoo! Finance. However, you can get it using the free Tick Data Downloader software. The program is very intuitive to use: just select the pairs and the time range you are interested in and click *Start download*.

Next you perform the simple calculations mentioned in *The Monthly Trade* section. I now use a proprietary program written in Python for this purpose but for years I did it with using Excel. I make my legacy Excel spreadsheet available at morbat.com/boexcel.

What asset should I trade each month?

That is a matter of personal preference. You could for example pick one index such as the SP-500 or a currency pair such as the EURUSD and stick to just trade that index or currency pair. If the size of your bankroll allows it, you could split it into two or more "virtual bankrolls" and trade different assets with each. That has the advantage of giving you some diversification. Another possibility is following a large number of assets and each month search for the trades with the higher expectancy. That is the approach I adopt.

Can you give an example of a set of trading rules?

Of course! A good trader has a set of trading rules he follows strictly. Here are Trader Ben rules:

1) Ben's bankroll is divided into four equally sized bankrolls. Bankroll #1 chases the highest expectancy trades for each month across all currencies; bankroll #2 chases the highest expectancy trades for each month across all indices; bankroll #3 trades the EURUSD and bankroll #4 trades the USDJPY.

2) Ben never overlaps trades. That means that with bankroll #1 Ben never trades the EURUSD or the USDJPY since these currency pairs are to be traded with bankrolls #3 and #4.

3) Ben only enters trades that have a winning percentage equal to or above 70%.

4) Ben uses the Kelly % to calculate how much to stake in each trade.

Which broker do you recommend?

The Calends strategy can be traded with any broker offering the binary options contracts mentioned (Higher/Lower or Rise/Fall) with at least one month duration. My broker of choice is Binary.com. Formerly called *BetOnMarkets*, they have been around for a very long time. Withdrawing money is an easy, fast and totally automatic process that does not require phone calls to a so called "account manager" whose only objective is to convince you to cancel your withdrawal request. I usually fund and withdraw using Skrill.

How much money do I need to trade with this strategy?

If you use ¼ of *The Kelly Percentage* or 2% of the *Percentage of Bankroll* a minimum of 100 euros will do although 500 or 1000 euros is certainly preferable. In any case always stick to your own money: never, ever borrow to trade.

Can someone do the trades for me?

If you do not have the time or for any other reason prefer not to trade yourself please go to morbat.com/calendstrader to receive information about available options.

Meet the Author

José Manuel Moreira Batista is a private trader and investor and manages private concerns. After graduating in Business Administration in 1982 he did a stint in the Air Force and then went on to hold executive positions in several multinational corporations until 1999.

That year he left the corporate world and started the management consulting and training company that he still owns today. He also taught university courses in Corporate Finance, Financial Accounting, Cost Accounting and Real Estate.

His results-oriented books and courses blend experience with a sound theoretical foundation to deliver practical, easy-to-follow knowledge that brings immediate benefits to readers and students. He lives in Cascais, Portugal.

Disclaimer

The author, publisher and related websites (collectively referred to as "Company") make no representations as to the accuracy, completeness, suitability or validity of any information in this book and will not be liable for any errors or omissions in this information or any damages arising from its display or use. The Company is neither providing investment advisory services nor acting as registered investment advisors or broker-dealers; they also do not purport to tell or suggest which securities or currencies customers should buy or sell for themselves. The Company may hold positions in the stocks, currencies or industries discussed here. You understand and acknowledge that there is a very high degree of risk involved in trading securities and/or currencies and/or options and/or CFD's and/or binary options. The Company assumes no responsibility or liability for your trading and investment results. Factual statements on the Company's website, or in its publications, are made as of the date stated and are subject to change without notice.

It should not be assumed that the methods, techniques, or indicators presented in these products will be profitable or that they will not result in losses. Past results of any individual trader or trading system published or mentioned by Company are not indicative of future returns by that trader or system, and are not indicative of future returns which be realized by you. In addition, the indicators, strategies, columns, articles, workbooks, spreadsheets, and all other features of Company's products (collectively, the "Information") are provided for informational and educational purposes only and should not be construed as investment advice. You should not rely solely on the Information in making any investment. Rather, you should use the Information only as a starting point for doing additional independent research in order to allow you to form your own opinion regarding investments.

You should always check with your licensed financial advisor and tax advisor to determine the suitability of any investment.

HYPOTHETICAL OR SIMULATED PERFORMANCE RESULTS HAVE CERTAIN INHERENT LIMITATIONS. UNLIKE AN ACTUAL PERFORMANCE RECORD, SIMULATED RESULTS DO NOT REPRESENT ACTUAL TRADING AND MAY NOT BE IMPACTED BY BROKERAGE AND OTHER SLIPPAGE FEES. ALSO, SINCE THE TRADES HAVE NOT ACTUALLY BEEN EXECUTED, THE RESULTS MAY HAVE UNDER- OR OVER-COMPENSATED FOR THE IMPACT, IF ANY, OF CERTAIN MARKET FACTORS, SUCH AS LACK OF LIQUIDITY. SIMULATED TRADING PROGRAMS IN GENERAL ARE ALSO SUBJECT TO THE FACT THAT THEY ARE DESIGNED WITH THE BENEFIT OF HINDSIGHT. NO REPRESENTATION IS BEING MADE THAT ANY ACCOUNT WILL OR IS LIKELY TO ACHIEVE PROFITS OR LOSSES SIMILAR TO THOSE SHOWN.

The Company may have an affiliate relationship with all or some of the companies whose products or services we mention. This means that, at no additional cost to you, Company may earn a commission or credit if you decide to buy any of their products or services.